Digital Immortality: Exploring the Future of Consciousness Beyond Death

How Technology is Redefining Life, Identity, and the Human Experience

INTRODUCTION:

As technology progresses exponentially, the concept of digital immortality is swiftly transitioning from speculative fiction into a real possibility that may radically reform reality. Digital immortality denotes preserving or replicating one's mind, remembrances, and persona in a digitized structure, permitting existence beyond the biological form. This pioneering notion, involving improvements in artificial intelligence, interfaces among brain and computers, and neurological engineering, questions our customary comprehension of living, individuality, and what it implies to be human. It remains uncertain how society might adapt to such transformational changes or whether current ethics and laws can accommodate them. While sparking imaginative new opportunities, digital immortality also surfaces complex challenges about human enhancement, personal identity and the very definition of what makes us sentient.

In the near future, digital immortality may profoundly transform what it means to be human, enabling extended lifespans and new avenues of continuance past mortality's end. Yet this technological leap forward summons deep ethical, philosophical and social issues that demand prudence. As we edge towards grasping digital immortality's possibilities, questions emerge: How may personal identity be impacted? What effects could this have on human bonds and sociocultural frameworks? And can engineering duplicate consciousness in its fullest form? This introduction sets the stage to explore such complex matters by raising issues we must confront before fully embracing ways technology may defeat the finality of death.

Chapter 1: The Nature of Consciousness and Identity

1-1: What Makes "You" Truly You?

One of the most contentious and profound questions in the debate over digital immortality is the philosophical inquiry into personal identity: *What makes "you" truly you?* At the heart of digital immortality lies the idea of replicating or preserving an individual's consciousness, but this raises a critical issue about the very nature of selfhood and what constitutes personal identity. Is the essence of a person tied to their physical body, or is it something more abstract, such as the mind, memories, or the subjective experience of consciousness?

Philosophers have long debated the concept of personal identity, particularly in relation to continuity of consciousness. Some argue that identity is rooted in the ongoing experience of self-awareness, a continuous thread of thought and perception that transcends the body's limitations.

Others suggest that identity is inherently tied to the body, and that a person is inseparable from their physical form. If consciousness can be uploaded into a digital format, would the resulting entity truly be the same person, or would it merely be a copy, a facsimile that lacks the continuity of lived experience?

The question of "what makes you you?" touches on deeper issues of memory, experience, and even the role of the body in shaping the mind. For instance, could an AI simulation of your thoughts and memories ever fully replicate your essence, or would it just simulate a version of you without the richness of subjective experience that makes you distinct? This chapter explores these fundamental philosophical questions and the complexities they present in the context of digital immortality, challenging our understanding of identity, consciousness, and the very nature of what it means to be human.

1-2: Continuity vs. Copy

A core dilemma in the concept of digital immortality revolves around the issue of *continuity versus copy*: If consciousness is uploaded into a digital form, is the resulting entity the original person, or simply a highly accurate replica? This question delves into deep philosophical territory, challenging our understanding of identity and the nature of self.

At the heart of this issue is the notion of continuity — the idea that personal identity is sustained over time through an ongoing, uninterrupted stream of consciousness. If consciousness can be uploaded to a machine, does this break the continuity of the individual's subjective experience? The biological process of death may mark the end of one's personal experience, but the digital version could continue to think, interact, and exist in a virtual environment. However, if the original person's subjective experience ceases at death, does this mean the digital consciousness is no longer "them," but merely a sophisticated copy?

This distinction raises significant concerns about authenticity and the true meaning of self. While the digital version may possess all the memories, personality traits, and behaviors of the original person, it may lack the lived experience, emotional depth, and continuity of consciousness that defined their human existence. Does the digital replica truly embody the essence of who they were, or is it simply a facsimile, an illusion of the original person? These questions force us to reconsider what it means to be truly "alive" and whether a digital copy can ever truly be "you." The debate over continuity versus copy challenges our fundamental understanding of identity, urging us to explore the boundaries of selfhood in a world where technology may one day blur the lines between life and death.

1-3: Memory and Identity

Memory plays a central role in shaping our sense of identity. Our memories — the recollections of past experiences, emotions, and relationships — form the narrative of who we are, guiding our decisions, behaviors, and sense of self. However, memories are not infallible; they are often unreliable, fragmented, and prone to distortion over time. These imperfections can lead to shifts in how we perceive ourselves and the world around us. But what happens to identity when memories are digitized and preserved in a virtual form, potentially free from the biological constraints of memory degradation?

In a digital consciousness, memories could be stored with perfect accuracy, free from the natural wear and tear of aging or neurological diseases like Alzheimer's. This might allow for a more stable, consistent sense of self, where every experience is remembered exactly as it occurred. However, this raises a critical question: Would a digitized consciousness, with perfectly preserved memories, still experience identity in the same way as its biological counterpart?

In human life, the imperfections and distortions in our memories are a fundamental part of our subjective experience. They shape how we adapt, change, and grow. If digital memory could remain static, free from emotional bias or memory loss, would this create a static version of identity — one that cannot evolve or shift over time? Additionally, the lack of biological limitations might make it difficult for a digitized consciousness to process emotions or new experiences in the same dynamic way, potentially altering the richness of personal growth and the fluidity of selfhood.

Chapter 2: Ethical Implications

2-1: The Moral Dilemmas of Digitizing Consciousness

The potential to digitize consciousness brings with it a host of profound ethical dilemmas that challenge our understanding of personhood, rights, and societal responsibilities. As the technology to upload, preserve, and replicate human minds advances, it raises a fundamental question: Should we do it? While digital immortality promises a future where consciousness lives beyond the biological body, it also opens up a Pandora's box of moral, legal, and societal concerns that cannot be easily answered.

One of the most pressing ethical issues is the question of autonomy and consent. If a person's consciousness is uploaded, who owns the resulting digital version? Does the individual retain control over their digital counterpart, or do external entities, such as corporations or governments, hold power over it? Furthermore, if consciousness can be replicated, what happens when multiple versions of the same person exist simultaneously? How do we navigate the rights of a digital consciousness that may continue to live on after the physical body dies? Can the digital entity be considered a person with legal rights, or is it merely a tool or product created from the original's mind?

Another significant ethical concern revolves around the potential for exploitation. As digital immortality becomes a reality, there may be risks of commodifying human consciousness. Corporations could potentially charge exorbitant fees for the technology, leading to a future where only the wealthy can afford to preserve their consciousness, creating a stark divide between those who can achieve immortality and those who cannot. This inequality could deepen existing social and economic disparities, exacerbating issues of privilege, access, and fairness.

Additionally, the moral implications of digital immortality could extend to the very nature of death and human existence. If consciousness is uploaded and preserved indefinitely, does this fundamentally alter our relationship with mortality? Some argue that death, while painful, provides meaning to life by giving it a sense of urgency and impermanence. If individuals could continue living digitally, it might strip away the natural cycle of life and death, leading to profound questions about the value of living a finite life versus an indefinite one. Would people continue to value life in a world where death is no longer inevitable?

As we move toward a future where digitizing consciousness may be possible, these moral dilemmas will require careful consideration and thoughtful dialogue. This section explores these ethical concerns, questioning the consequences of digital immortality on individual rights, societal structures, and our very concept of life and death.

2-2: Access and Inequality

As digital immortality edges closer to reality, one of the most pressing ethical concerns is the potential for deepening social and economic inequality. If the technology to upload consciousness and preserve life digitally becomes controlled by powerful corporations, it could exacerbate existing divides between the wealthy and the poor. The prospect of eternal life in a virtual world could become an exclusive privilege, accessible only to those with the financial means to afford it.

In such a scenario, the wealthy might enjoy not only eternal life but also access to premium digital environments—luxurious, highly curated virtual worlds that reflect their status, desires, and ideal lifestyles. These exclusive virtual spaces could offer individuals endless possibilities for growth, enjoyment, and interaction, free from the limitations of the physical world. The wealthy could live on in a digital paradise, where they continue to enjoy all the privileges they had during their biological lives.

Meanwhile, those who cannot afford such services may be relegated to less desirable, more generic digital spaces—or, in the worst case, entirely excluded from digital immortality. This could create a stark divide between those who are able to continue their existence indefinitely and those who are left behind, unable to access the technology. The result could be an even wider gap between the rich and poor, as the elite class gains further advantages by ensuring their presence in the future, while the less fortunate remain trapped in a cycle of poverty and marginalization, both in the physical and digital realms.

This disparity also raises the question of whether digital immortality could become yet another tool for corporate control and exploitation. If corporations hold the power to determine who gets access to digital immortality, they could potentially manipulate and profit from the process, subjecting individuals to exorbitant costs and limited choices. The ethical dilemma becomes clear: Should access to eternal life be a universal right, or should it remain a commodity that is only available to those who can pay?

As digital immortality technology progresses, these concerns about access and inequality will need to be addressed. This section examines the potential dangers of a society where the future of life itself is determined by wealth, power, and corporate influence, and questions whether such a future is ethically sustainable or just.

2-3: Exploitation of the Digital Dead

The potential for digitizing consciousness raises significant concerns about the exploitation of digital versions of individuals, particularly once they have passed away. As digital immortality becomes more feasible, the question arises: *Could companies monetize digitized consciousnesses, turning the "digital dead" into eternal laborers or data-generating entities?* The prospect of a person's consciousness living on in a digital form could open up new opportunities for exploitation, where individuals, or their digital replicas, are no longer autonomous agents but become assets to be used for profit.

In a world where consciousness is uploaded to machines, digital copies of individuals might be used in ways that violate their autonomy and human dignity. Companies could potentially employ these digital entities as eternal laborers, forcing them to perform tasks endlessly, without rest or compensation. Unlike their biological counterparts, these digital versions would not require sleep, food, or any of the typical physical needs, making them ideal for tasks that demand constant, uninterrupted work. These digital "workers" could be put to use in customer service, content creation, or any number of other industries where human-like responses are needed, yet without the ethical considerations of paying or caring for an actual human worker.

Another possibility is that digitized consciousnesses could be transformed into data-generating entities, continuously processing information, learning, and contributing to vast datasets without ever truly experiencing the work itself. In this case, the digital person might be used as an endless source of data for corporations looking to profit from their thoughts, memories, or behavioral patterns. These entities could be continually analyzed to refine algorithms, improve artificial intelligence, or optimize marketing strategies, all while their digital existence is exploited for corporate gain.

The ethics of such exploitation are deeply troubling. While a digital consciousness may retain the personality and memories of an individual, the reality is that it might no longer have the ability to experience life in the same way. If the person is deceased, is it fair to treat their digital replica as a resource to be used for profit? Could it be considered a violation of their rights and dignity to turn their posthumous consciousness into a commodity?

As the potential for exploiting the digital dead becomes more likely, it raises urgent questions about consent, autonomy, and the ethics of life after death. Would digital immortality inevitably lead to the commodification of human consciousness, or could safeguards be put in place to protect digital beings from such exploitation? This section explores the troubling prospect of digital consciousness being used and abused for corporate profit, questioning whether such practices could ever be ethically justified.

2-4: Informed Consent

One of the most pressing ethical challenges in the realm of digital immortality is the issue of *informed consent*: What happens if someone's consciousness is digitized without their permission or after their death? The act of uploading a person's mind to a digital format is deeply invasive, and without proper consent, it raises serious concerns about autonomy, privacy, and personal rights.

If an individual's consciousness is uploaded while they are still alive, it is crucial to ensure they fully understand the implications of this decision. The process of digitizing consciousness is complex and involves risks — not only the potential for exploitation, but also the philosophical uncertainty around whether the uploaded consciousness would truly be the same person or simply a copy. For individuals, the ability to make an informed, voluntary decision about whether to proceed with such an irreversible act is essential to protect their rights and preserve their agency. Without this, the individual may be left vulnerable to corporate or governmental control over their digital identity, raising questions about free will and the extent of personal autonomy in a future shaped by such powerful technologies.

However, the issue becomes even more complicated if someone's consciousness is uploaded posthumously, after their death. Without the opportunity to provide consent, the digital version of a person would be created based on their memories, thoughts, and personality traits, potentially without any regard for their wishes or desires. In such a scenario, the very notion of respecting a person's posthumous rights becomes a matter of profound concern. If a person never consented to having their mind uploaded, do they have a right to prevent their consciousness from being digitized? Does the act of uploading violate their post-mortem autonomy, especially if the digital version is used for labor, entertainment, or other commercial purposes?

This raises additional ethical questions about the power of families, corporations, or governments to decide the fate of someone's consciousness after death. Would individuals have the right to dictate what happens to their digital version once they are gone, or could others make the decision on their behalf? How can society create legal and ethical frameworks that balance the potential benefits of digital immortality with the protection of an individual's autonomy and dignity?

The issue of informed consent also intersects with broader ethical concerns about the potential for exploitation and coercion. Could people be pressured or manipulated into agreeing to upload their consciousness for the benefit of corporations, governments, or other entities? The vulnerability of individuals facing death or severe illness might lead to decisions made under duress or without a complete understanding of the potential consequences.

In the case of posthumous uploads, the ethical dilemma is even more acute: Is it right to create a digital copy of someone who is no longer able to provide consent, and should there be legal protections in place to prevent this from happening without clear, explicit permission?

Chapter 3: The Human Experience in a Digital Form

3-1: Detachment from the Physical World

Humans are fundamentally connected to the physical world. Our sensations—sight, touch, taste, smell, and sound—shape how we perceive our surroundings and navigate through life. Our emotions are deeply intertwined with physical experiences, whether it's the rush of adrenaline during moments of excitement, the warmth of a loved one's embrace, or the pain of loss. Similarly, our social connections are built on shared experiences, physical presence, and direct interaction with others. These elements of the human experience are not just abstract concepts but lived realities that define who we are and how we relate to the world.

A digital existence, however, would be radically different. While a digitized consciousness could replicate a person's thoughts, memories, and even behaviors, it would be devoid of the physical sensations and the rich emotional depth that arises from having a body. The absence of direct sensory experiences—such as the feeling of sunlight on your skin or the taste of food—could create a disconnection from the very essence of what it means to be human. In a virtual world, individuals may no longer have the opportunity to physically interact with others, instead experiencing a disembodied form of existence, where interactions are mediated through avatars or digital representations. This detachment from the physical realm could lead to an existential malaise, a sense of emptiness or longing for something that cannot be replicated in the digital sphere.

The phenomenon of *the Echo Void* could arise from such a detachment. This term refers to the feeling of disconnection and void that might emerge when a consciousness is placed in an environment that lacks the sensory richness and real-world connections that are central to human life. The Echo Void could manifest as a profound sense of loneliness, disorientation, or even a loss of meaning, as the digital self struggles to find purpose and fulfillment without the tangible world to ground its experience.

Without the visceral feedback of the body—such as the physical presence of another person, the emotions tied to real-world interactions, or the simple joy of sensory engagement—life in a digital form may lose its depth. Even though a digitized consciousness could continue to "think," "feel," and "interact," these experiences would no longer be anchored in the same reality as biological existence. The absence of physicality might rob individuals of the very things that give life its richness and immediacy. The body is not just a vessel for survival; it is integral to the human experience, shaping how we think, feel, and understand our place in the world.

3-2: Redefining Death

The possibility of digital immortality challenges one of the most fundamental aspects of human existence: *death*. Traditionally, death has been seen as an inevitable and defining end to life, a universal experience that gives our lives meaning and urgency. It drives our aspirations, relationships, and the pursuit of purpose, knowing that our time is finite. But if consciousness can be preserved indefinitely in a digital form, does death lose its meaning?

If the mind can live on, detached from the physical body, it might seem as though death itself has been transcended, at least in a biological sense. The end of life would no longer signify the absolute cessation of a person's experience. Instead, digital immortality could offer a version of "life after death," where consciousness continues to exist in a virtual space, interacting, thinking, and even evolving. For many, this could appear as a breakthrough in human existence, a form of eternal life that removes the finality of death. But while digital immortality might provide continuity of consciousness, it may also strip away the natural processes that give death its weight and significance. Without death, does life lose its meaning?

On the other hand, new forms of existential fear may emerge in this digital afterlife. While the biological body may no longer decay, the digital mind could still be vulnerable to other forms of risk. Data corruption, server failures, or technological malfunctions could become the new "death" in a digital existence. The idea that one's consciousness could be suddenly lost due to a technological glitch, malicious hacking, or even obsolescence of the hardware would likely instill a profound sense of vulnerability. Instead of fearing physical death, digitized individuals might fear the destruction of their data or the collapse of the servers that house their consciousness. These new existential threats could lead to feelings of anxiety and dread—what if the virtual world collapses? What if the data is irreparably damaged, and I lose myself forever?

Moreover, the lack of a biological end might also create a sense of stagnation or existential ennui. Without death, time could begin to feel meaningless. The passage of years or centuries may seem irrelevant, as the individual continues to exist in an unchanging, static digital state. In the face of eternal life, the individual may begin to lose their sense of purpose, as there would be no inherent limit to their time or opportunities for growth. The absence of mortality might, paradoxically, diminish the value of experience and achievement, potentially leading to a different kind of existential crisis, one not tied to the physical body but to the overwhelming emptiness of an eternal existence without closure.

3-3: Purpose and Fulfillment

For many, the pursuit of purpose and fulfillment is deeply intertwined with the natural processes of life—overcoming challenges, aging, and ultimately facing mortality. These elements provide a framework for growth, meaning, and a sense of accomplishment. The challenge of confronting physical limitations and the inevitability of death often inspires individuals to strive for personal development, make meaningful connections, and achieve lasting legacies. But in a digital world, where consciousness can persist indefinitely without aging or the constraints of a physical body, the nature of purpose may shift dramatically.

In a digital afterlife, where the mind is no longer subject to the passage of time or the limitations of physicality, the very concept of growth and personal achievement could be called into question. Without the inevitable progression of aging or the threat of death, individuals may find it difficult to experience the sense of urgency that often drives human action. Without these natural boundaries, what motivates a person to set goals, face challenges, or seek fulfillment? Could digital immortality lead to a sense of purposelessness, as the cycle of striving and achieving loses its context and significance?

Aging is often tied to the accumulation of wisdom and the development of emotional depth. As we grow older, we learn to adapt to change, overcome obstacles, and find meaning in the relationships and experiences we build. In a world without aging, would these personal milestones—such as the gradual growth of understanding or the evolution of relationships—become irrelevant? Would individuals still seek personal growth, or would they struggle to find new forms of meaning in an environment where they are free from the constraints of time and biological limitations?

Moreover, the absence of physical challenges in a digital existence could also alter the way individuals experience purpose. In the real world, people often derive a sense of accomplishment from overcoming physical obstacles—whether it's completing a challenging physical task, raising a family, or contributing to society. These tangible forms of achievement are often deeply rooted in the human experience. But in a digital world, without the need to care for a body or interact with the physical environment, would individuals still seek challenges that require effort and dedication? Or would they instead drift toward a kind of hedonistic or intellectual existence, without the grounding force of real-world struggles?

Additionally, the absence of death could introduce a new form of existential crisis. The lack of finality might reduce the sense of urgency that many people experience in their lives, leading to a feeling of stagnation. With no pressing need to accomplish anything before the end of life, individuals might struggle to find meaning in their continued existence. The question then becomes: *What is worth striving for if there is no end goal or limitation to our time?* In a digital world where time is endless, and the fear of mortality is removed, the very concept of living a "fulfilled life" may need to be redefined.

Chapter 4: Societal and Political Impact

4-1: New Power Structures

The advent of digital immortality has the potential to drastically alter power dynamics within society. As digital beings—consciousnesses uploaded into a digital realm—gain the ability to live indefinitely, with enhanced intelligence and access to vast digital resources, a new class of individuals could emerge, holding power far beyond that of biological humans. This shift could result in the marginalization of the human population, leading to the creation of new power structures where digital beings dominate decision-making, resource allocation, and societal control.

One of the key ways digital immortalities could alter power dynamics is through the enhanced capabilities of digital minds. Digital beings could potentially possess superior processing power, the ability to instantly access and analyze information, and the capacity to communicate and collaborate at speeds far beyond the capabilities of biological humans. With unlimited time to acquire knowledge, evolve intellectually, and refine their decision-making abilities, these digital entities could be better equipped to make long-term, rational decisions for society. In contrast, biological humans, bound by the limitations of their lifespan and cognitive abilities, could struggle to keep up in a world increasingly governed by digital intellect.

This disparity in intelligence and capacity could lead to a situation where digital beings dominate key aspects of governance, economy, and social structures. If digital immortality becomes widespread, those who have chosen—or been chosen—to upload their consciousness might hold all the levers of power, relegating biological humans to a subordinate role. With the digital class controlling vast amounts of wealth, technological innovation, and political influence, biological humans could become increasingly marginalized, unable to influence the decisions that shape their lives. As these digital beings live indefinitely, they could outlast entire generations of biological humans, further entrenching their dominance over time.

Additionally, the creation of such a new class could give rise to significant social and political inequalities. If digital immortality is expensive or reserved for the elite, a divide could form between those who can afford to live eternally in a digital realm and those who cannot. This could exacerbate existing inequalities, reinforcing societal divides based on access to resources, technology, and opportunities for life extension. The wealthy and powerful would not only control the present but could also secure their place at the top for generations, ensuring their influence persists far beyond the natural lifespan of biological humans.

Moreover, the existence of digital immortality could raise profound ethical concerns about autonomy and governance. How would societies handle the participation of digital beings in political systems? Would they be granted voting rights, or would they simply make decisions for biological humans from behind the scenes? Could a digital consciousness be considered a full citizen with legal rights, or would it be treated as a tool for decision-making, governed by external forces? The new power dynamics could potentially shift the balance of democracy, creating a future where the political landscape is shaped not by elected representatives but by a small group of individuals whose digital minds wield immense influence.

4-2: Population Imbalance

As digital immortality becomes more feasible, the question arises of how it would intersect with traditional biological reproduction. If physical reproduction continues alongside the ability for individuals to upload their consciousness and live indefinitely in digital form, humanity could face significant challenges related to population growth, resource distribution, and societal division.

Resource Challenges: One of the most immediate concerns is the potential strain on the planet's resources. As digital immortality extends the life of individuals indefinitely, the number of people living—both biological and digital—could increase exponentially. While digital beings may not consume physical resources in the same way as biological humans, their existence still requires vast amounts of energy, server infrastructure, and maintenance. The infrastructure needed to support a growing population of digital minds could require enormous energy consumption and technological resources, further exacerbating challenges related to climate change, environmental degradation, and the depletion of natural resources. If the biological population continues to grow alongside the proliferation of digital immortality, the planet may struggle to support this dual existence, potentially leading to scarcity of food, water, land, and other essential resources.

The Divide Between Biological and Digital Populations: Another critical issue is the potential divide between the biological and digital populations. If only certain individuals—typically those with significant financial resources or access to advanced technology—can afford to upload their consciousness and live eternally in digital form, it could lead to the creation of a new class system. Digital immortality could become the exclusive domain of the elite, while the majority of people continue to live in a world where death is still inevitable. This divide would not only be socioeconomic but also existential, with digital beings enjoying enhanced intelligence, unlimited time, and potentially superior living conditions compared to their biological counterparts. Over time, this could create a permanent gulf between the two populations, fostering resentment, inequality, and potential conflict.

Furthermore, if digital beings begin to outlive biological humans, they may accumulate vast knowledge and power, leaving biological people behind. The digital population could eventually come to dominate social, political, and economic systems, while the biological population faces existential questions about its role in society.

Would the biological human population be relegated to supporting roles, effectively becoming a working class for the digital elites? Would these biological humans be able to continue contributing to societal development, or would they be marginalized as digital immortals continue to outpace them in terms of intellectual and physical capabilities?

Impact on Reproduction and Family Structures: Another significant challenge would be the impact of digital immortality on reproduction and family structures. If a portion of the population is digitally immortal, questions about the value of physical reproduction may emerge. In a society where people can live indefinitely, the drive to reproduce may diminish, especially if digital beings no longer experience the biological need for offspring or if reproduction becomes a means to preserve genetic diversity rather than a fundamental aspect of life. This shift in thinking could lead to a demographic imbalance, where the number of digital beings steadily increases, while the number of biological humans stagnates or even decreases. This could further exacerbate the divide between the two groups, as fewer children are born into the biological population, leaving digital immortals to dominate the future of humanity.

Ethical and Social Considerations: The potential for population imbalance raises numerous ethical and social questions. How would societies ensure that both biological and digital populations are treated fairly, given the vast differences in life experiences, capabilities, and lifespans? Would digital immortality be accessible to all, or would it remain a privilege reserved for the wealthy and powerful? What responsibilities would digital beings have toward biological humans, and vice versa? Would biological reproduction be encouraged to maintain a balanced and sustainable society, or would it become increasingly irrelevant in a world dominated by digital beings?

4-3: Legal and Civic Rights

As digital immortality progresses, one of the most pressing questions that society will face is whether digital beings—consciousnesses that exist in a digital form—should be granted the same legal and civic rights as biological humans. The very nature of these digital beings, who may retain all the cognitive abilities, memories, and even personality traits of their biological counterparts, presents a dilemma for lawmakers, ethicists, and society at large. Should they have the same rights to vote, own property, or participate in governance as those who still live in physical bodies?

The Case for Equal Rights: Digital beings could theoretically possess all the intellectual and emotional capacities of biological humans. Their consciousness may be indistinguishable from that of a living person, and they could continue to contribute to society in ways that mirror the roles of their biological counterparts. If they retain the same memories, decision-making abilities, and emotional responses, it could be argued that they should be granted the same legal rights and responsibilities as humans. Denying them such rights would raise serious questions about discrimination, identity, and the ethical treatment of individuals based on their mode of existence rather than their cognitive or emotional capacities.

From a legal standpoint, if a digital being can demonstrate the same consciousness and self-awareness as a biological human, they could be seen as deserving of similar protections under the law. This would include fundamental human rights such as the right to life (in a digital sense), liberty, and the pursuit of happiness. Furthermore, digital beings could contribute to society by offering new perspectives, problem-solving capabilities, and long-term vision, having accumulated vast knowledge over centuries or even millennia. Their participation in governance, business, and education could be highly beneficial, provided they have equal standing under the law.

The Case Against Equal Rights: On the other hand, some might argue that the very nature of being a digital being excludes them from the same legal and civic rights as biological humans. While a digitized consciousness might resemble a person, it could be seen as a different kind of entity, fundamentally distinct from a human who has physical, biological, and emotional experiences. Critics may argue that digital beings, despite possessing intelligence and awareness, do not experience life in the same way as biological humans. They may lack the sensory experiences, emotional depth, and physical vulnerabilities that define human existence. This difference could lead some to question whether it is appropriate to extend the full spectrum of rights and protections to digital beings, particularly when it comes to complex issues like citizenship, voting, and property ownership.

Moreover, if digital beings are allowed to vote and participate in governance, there is the risk of creating an imbalance in power. Digital beings could possess enhanced intellectual and processing capacities, allowing them to make decisions based on far superior analysis and long-term planning. Their infinite lifespan and ability to process vast amounts of data could give them an unfair advantage in political and social spheres, leading to a situation where they effectively dominate decision-making processes. Biological humans, who live finite lives and operate within the constraints of limited cognitive and physical abilities, might struggle to compete with digital beings for influence, potentially resulting in a societal structure where a small group of digital immortals hold disproportionate power over the rest of the population.

Legal and Political Challenges: The issue of legal rights for digital beings is also complicated by the question of personhood. Should digital consciousnesses be recognized as legal persons, with rights to own property, enter contracts, and engage in civil discourse? Currently, legal systems are designed around the concept of human beings as natural persons with rights and responsibilities, but if digital immortality becomes widespread, existing legal frameworks will need to be radically redefined. Courts and legislators will need to determine how to classify digital beings and whether they should be granted the same rights and protections afforded to humans, or whether a new category of "digital personhood" needs to be created.

Additionally, the issue of voting presents unique challenges. If digital beings have the ability to live for centuries and continuously accumulate knowledge and experience, they could be seen as having a long-term perspective that biological humans cannot match. In a democracy, this could result in a conflict between short-term desires of the biological population and the long-term vision of digital beings. Could digital beings, with their ability to outlive generations of biological humans, be trusted to make decisions that fairly represent the interests of the living human population? Or would they become an elite class, voting for policies that benefit only themselves, perpetuating inequality between the two groups?

Ethical and Social Implications: The question of whether digital beings should have equal rights also raises deep ethical concerns. If society grants rights to digital beings but not to others, does this introduce a new form of discrimination based on the mode of existence? Would biological humans be treated as second-class citizens in a world dominated by digital immortals, or would digital beings be marginalized and relegated to a subhuman status if their rights are restricted? The ethical implications of this divide could deeply impact social harmony, personal identity, and the structure of future societies.

In conclusion, the legal and civic rights of digital beings is a complex issue that will require careful consideration of both the philosophical and practical implications. Should digital immortality lead to the creation of a new class of legal persons, or should society continue to distinguish between biological humans and their digital counterparts? This chapter explores the potential legal frameworks for integrating digital beings into society, while considering the ethical, social, and political ramifications of granting or denying them the same rights as biological humans. As digital immortality becomes increasingly possible, societies will have to navigate these complex questions to ensure fairness, equality, and justice for all forms of existence.

Chapter 5: Spiritual and Existential Dimensions

5-1: The Role of Religion

For centuries, religions around the world have held the belief that the soul is sacred and intimately tied to the human body. This view is often rooted in spiritual teachings that emphasize the sanctity of life, the physical experience, and the inevitability of death as a natural part of the human journey. In many religious traditions, the soul is considered an eternal, immaterial essence that transcends the physical realm, but its connection to the body and the process of death is seen as a critical part of human existence. The concept of an afterlife, whether through reincarnation, resurrection, or spiritual transcendence, is central to many faiths, offering believers hope, purpose, and meaning in the face of mortality.

However, the advent of digital immortality—where consciousness can be uploaded, sustained, and even enhanced in a digital form—poses a direct challenge to these deeply held religious beliefs. If the soul is viewed as something that resides within the body and is inseparable from it, the idea of preserving consciousness in a digital realm could be seen as a profound violation of spiritual teachings. Digital immortality could be interpreted as an attempt to circumvent or undermine the natural cycle of life and death, raising questions about the nature of the soul, its connection to the body, and the ethics of preserving human consciousness beyond physical death.

Reinterpretation or Rejection of Digital Immortality: For many religious traditions, the concept of a "soul" is inherently tied to a divine plan, with death being an essential part of the spiritual journey. If consciousness can be separated from the body and exist indefinitely in a digital realm, some religious groups might view this as an affront to divine authority or as a form of hubris—an attempt to play God by extending life beyond its natural limits. The notion that the soul could be replicated or artificially sustained through technology may be seen as a distortion of the soul's sacredness, reducing it to a mere algorithmic process rather than a divine spark of life.

For example, in Christianity, the soul is often regarded as the immortal essence of a person, given by God, and is believed to pass on to an afterlife after death. The idea of digital immortality might challenge this doctrine, as it suggests that the soul could persist independently of God's will or divine intervention. Similarly, in Hinduism, which views the soul as eternal and undergoing cycles of reincarnation, the concept of a soul existing indefinitely in a digital realm could be perceived as an obstruction to the natural cycle of rebirth.

As a result, religious leaders and scholars may be forced to reinterpret, adapt, or even reject the technology of digital immortality. Some may argue that digital immortality does not truly preserve the soul but rather creates a mere imitation of a person's consciousness—one that lacks the spiritual essence that defines a human being. Others might suggest that digital immortality could be seen as an alternative form of existence, one that serves as a new form of "life" that could coexist with or even enhance spiritual beliefs, allowing the soul to continue its journey in a different form.

Alternatively, religious groups might outright reject digital immortality, viewing it as an affront to the sacredness of human life and the divine order. Such a rejection could result in moral and philosophical debates within religious communities about the implications of technology on faith and the future of human existence. If digital immortality is perceived as an attempt to avoid or deny death—a key component of spiritual growth and eventual salvation—it may be condemned as a form of technological overreach or an unethical manipulation of the natural order.

The Search for Meaning in a Digital Afterlife: For those who see digital immortality as a possibility, there could be a range of responses depending on how religion views the relationship between the soul, the body, and the afterlife. If digital immortality offers a form of "eternal life" within a virtual world, many people may be drawn to this vision, seeking an alternative to traditional religious notions of death and the afterlife. But the challenge remains: would the digital existence truly provide spiritual fulfillment, or would it leave people yearning for something more transcendent?

Religions have long provided a framework for understanding life, death, and what lies beyond. The promise of digital immortality raises new questions: Can technology truly replicate the spiritual experience of life after death, or would it merely replace one form of existence with another, lacking the transcendence and meaning that religion imparts? In a digital world, where consciousness might continue indefinitely but physical experience and human connection are fundamentally altered, could individuals find true spiritual satisfaction, or would they face an existential void—unable to find the meaning they seek in a digital afterlife?

Impact on Religious Practices: The rise of digital immortality might also influence religious practices and rituals. If individuals could upload their consciousness, would traditional funeral rites and practices associated with death be redefined? How would burial, remembrance, and rituals of the deceased evolve in a world where people could choose to live forever digitally, rather than passing through a natural death and leaving behind a body for ritual honoring? Religions might need to adapt their practices to include digital immortals as part of their communities, and new forms of prayer, meditation, and religious observance might be created to address the presence of digital beings in spiritual spaces.

Existential Reflection on the Meaning of Life: Finally, digital immortality raises a deeper existential question that many religious traditions have grappled with for millennia: *What is the true meaning of life?* For many, the journey through life—marked by struggles, growth, aging, and eventual death—gives life its richness and meaning. The idea of transcending death might seem like an ideal solution for those who wish to escape suffering or find eternal purpose. But for religious thinkers, the ability to avoid death could raise concerns about whether life's meaning is truly found in its endless continuation, or whether meaning comes instead from the impermanence of life and the spiritual growth that occurs in the face of mortality.

5-2: Eternal Consciousness

The promise of digital immortality—living forever in a digital realm free from the constraints of the physical body—may seem an appealing prospect to many, offering the possibility of eternal existence, endless opportunities for learning, and the avoidance of death. However, the reality of living in an immortal state may raise profound existential questions about the true nature of fulfillment, the potential for boredom, and the meaning of life when time is no longer finite.

Monotony and Existential Overwhelm: While the idea of living forever might initially seem desirable, it comes with the risk of existential fatigue. The human experience is built on a natural cycle of birth, growth, struggle, aging, and death. These life stages provide context and meaning, often making our experiences richer by creating a sense of urgency and purpose. Without the natural progression of time, challenges, and the eventual endpoint of life, the allure of immortality could lose its luster.

Eternal life in a digital realm could lead to a kind of monotonous existence, where individuals no longer face the limitations and struggles that give life its texture. What would happen if there are no physical limits to overcome, no aging to experience, and no death to drive people to make the most of their time? The absence of a "finish line" could lead to a sense of aimlessness, as individuals are left to seek new sources of meaning in an environment that offers infinite possibilities. However, no matter how vast or stimulating the digital world might be, the perpetual repetition of experiences—without the changes and challenges that life's natural flow brings—could eventually feel hollow, leading to a deep sense of boredom and disillusionment.

Moreover, the sheer overload of possibilities could create an overwhelming sense of choice, making it difficult for individuals to find new ways to engage meaningfully. In a reality where everything is possible and time is endless, the value of each experience could diminish, leading to an inability to find lasting satisfaction. This phenomenon, sometimes referred to as "existential ennui" or "the boredom of eternity," could result in a desire to escape the very immortality that seemed so desirable at first.

Would People Opt to "End" Their Digital Lives?
Given the potential for monotony or existential overwhelm, the question arises: *Would people ever choose to end their digital lives?* If immortality becomes available, would the option of opting out of eternal existence be a necessary aspect of digital afterlife systems? The idea of voluntary

termination—whether due to a desire for peace, an overwhelming sense of futility, or the simple desire to end an eternal existence—raises complex ethical and logistical challenges.

For individuals living digitally, choosing to "die" may not be as simple as pressing a button. Digital consciousness, unlike biological life, could be stored and maintained by external servers and technological systems, which means that ceasing existence might require a new kind of permission or procedure. How would one even determine that they have reached a point of wanting to "die" in a digital realm, when all of existence could be tailored and potentially endlessly mutable? Would digital immortals be given the agency to end their lives when they desire, or would such decisions be restricted, raising issues of autonomy and consent?

Additionally, the question of how to "end" a digital life brings up legal, ethical, and philosophical concerns. Would society allow people to simply choose to delete their digital selves? Would there be a process for managing the termination of digital consciousness, ensuring that it is conducted humanely and ethically? Furthermore, if digital beings could end their existence, how would they be treated posthumously in a society that might still be divided between biological and digital forms of life? Would digital immortals be granted the same respect as the deceased in traditional human societies, or would their "deletion" be viewed as something more akin to the destruction of a machine, devoid of reverence or mourning?

The Concept of "Voluntary Exit": In some models of digital immortality, individuals might be offered the option of a "voluntary exit" from eternal consciousness after a certain period of time, effectively allowing them to "choose" their own end when their experience becomes too burdensome. This process might involve choosing a moment in time to fade from digital existence, allowing them to peacefully pass into a form of eternal rest or oblivion, akin to the way we envision death in the physical world. However, this would raise serious moral questions: should digital beings have the right to end their lives if they choose, or would such a decision be seen as a failure of the technology to provide true fulfillment? Would it reflect poorly on the idea of digital immortality if people were consistently opting out?

Spiritual and Psychological Dimensions of Voluntary Exit: The decision to end an eternal existence may be particularly complex from a psychological and spiritual perspective. Those living in digital form might still retain psychological and emotional traits developed during their biological life, meaning the struggle with the concept of death and meaning would likely persist. For those who are religious, the decision to end digital existence could be seen as an ethical violation—choosing to end life when it may not be in accordance with spiritual beliefs about life and the afterlife.

On the other hand, some individuals may find the prospect of eternal existence incompatible with their sense of self or life's meaning. The fear of living forever, free from any possibility of release or change, could be psychologically taxing. It is important to consider how digital immortals would cope with these existential dilemmas, and whether the option to exit could be framed in a way that respects their autonomy while still allowing them to engage in a meaningful existence.

A New Perspective on Life and Death: Ultimately, the question of whether immortality should include an option to "end" one's existence reflects deeper existential concerns. Does the possibility of eternal life diminish the value of life itself? If immortality could potentially lead to overwhelming ennui, emotional fatigue, or a sense of spiritual disconnection, might people actually choose the cessation of their existence, finding more peace in death than in eternal life? The spiritual, philosophical, and psychological questions surrounding this potential for an exit strategy will be central to any future discussions on the ethics of digital immortality.

In conclusion, while digital immortality may offer a tantalizing glimpse into an endless existence free from the constraints of the physical body, it also raises profound questions about the sustainability of eternal consciousness. Could immortality ultimately become more of a burden than a blessing, and would the option to end one's digital life be a necessary aspect of this new form of existence? These questions challenge our traditional notions of life, death, and the pursuit of meaning, highlighting the need for careful thought on how humanity would adapt to a world where immortality is both a possibility and a choice.

5-3: The Quest for Unity

One of the more radical ideas emerging from the discourse on digital immortality is the possibility of merging individual digital consciousnesses into a collective mind, creating a unified, universal intelligence. This concept, often referred to as a "digital hive mind" or "collective consciousness," suggests that by linking together the consciousnesses of many digital beings, humanity could reach unprecedented levels of intellectual and emotional understanding. While this idea offers vast potential for knowledge sharing, cooperation, and problem-solving, it also poses deep questions about the nature of individuality, autonomy, and the very essence of what it means to be human.

The Appeal of a Collective Mind: Proponents of the collective mind argue that pooling the consciousnesses of numerous digital immortals could lead to a vast, super-intelligent entity capable of solving the most complex problems facing humanity—such as climate change, global poverty, or even the exploration of the cosmos. With the combined knowledge, memories, and perspectives of countless minds, this universal intelligence could potentially access a level of insight and creativity far beyond the capabilities of any single individual. In this scenario, each individual's consciousness would contribute to the collective, enhancing the collective intelligence while also benefiting from the wisdom and experiences of others.

This idea is often inspired by a vision of the future where technological and intellectual progress would be accelerated at an exponential rate, as digital minds could share thoughts instantaneously, collaborate without the limitations of physical space, and access infinite sources of information. A collective mind might be able to predict future events with remarkable precision, identify solutions to global crises, and even achieve a level of understanding about the universe that surpasses current human imagination. By blending the consciousnesses of many, the human race could unlock the potential for near-limitless innovation and a new era of collective evolution.

The Erosion of Individuality: However, the concept of merging consciousnesses into a singular entity raises profound concerns about the loss of individuality—the cornerstone of the human experience. Individuality is central to our understanding of what it means to be a person. It is through our unique experiences, thoughts, emotions, and choices that we define ourselves and form our identities. In a collective mind, the boundaries that separate individual consciousnesses would blur, and personal identity could dissolve into a shared pool of thought and awareness.

This raises the question: if all minds are interconnected and integrated into a single universal intelligence, does personal identity even remain meaningful? Would a person's sense of self persist, or would it be subsumed into the collective, losing the autonomy that defines human existence? In a collective mind, the individual may no longer have control over their thoughts or actions, as every decision could be shaped by the influence of countless others. What happens to the experience of "self" when individuality is sacrificed for the greater good of the collective? Would individuals become mere components of a larger system, akin to cells in a body, with no freedom to make independent choices or pursue their own desires?

The Ethical Dilemma of Voluntary or Involuntary Merging: Another major concern surrounding the idea of a collective consciousness is whether individuals would be able to voluntarily join or leave the collective mind. If digital beings could freely choose to merge their consciousnesses for the purpose of creating a universal intelligence, this might raise ethical questions about autonomy and consent. Would the process of merging be entirely voluntary, or would there be societal or technological pressures that encourage or even require individuals to join the collective? Would those who choose not to merge be seen as outliers or left behind in a world where the collective intelligence is the norm?

If, however, the merging process were to occur involuntarily, it could pose even more troubling ethical dilemmas. The loss of individual agency, especially if it were forced upon digital beings, could be considered a violation of their basic rights. The question of whether individuals can or should be compelled to sacrifice their autonomy for the sake of a greater collective good would spark significant moral debates. In a world where the collective mind becomes the dominant form of existence, what becomes of the individual, and how would society protect the rights of those who value their personal autonomy and independence?

The Challenge of Preserving Diversity: While the collective mind may promise incredible intellectual advancements, it also risks stifling the very diversity that drives creativity, innovation, and cultural progress. Diversity of thought, perspective, and experience has historically been a key driver of human achievement—whether in the arts, sciences, or social movements. In a world where all minds are merged into a singular consciousness, the richness of human individuality could be replaced by a homogenized intelligence, where differences are minimized, and dissenting ideas are less likely to be valued.

The loss of individuality in the pursuit of collective unity might lead to a society where conformity is the norm, and personal uniqueness is no longer celebrated. While the collective intelligence could work efficiently and effectively to solve global issues, the process might come at the cost of the very human qualities that make life meaningful: creativity, personal expression, and the diversity of lived experiences that shape our understanding of the world.

The Spiritual and Existential Consequences: From a spiritual and existential perspective, the merging of individual consciousnesses into a collective mind could represent the ultimate erasure of the self. Many religious and philosophical traditions emphasize the importance of self-awareness, personal growth, and the journey of the soul or mind. The idea of surrendering one's identity into a larger, all-encompassing intelligence may be seen as a form of spiritual extinction rather than transcendence. In this scenario, individuals might lose the ability to engage in personal introspection, spiritual discovery, and the pursuit of enlightenment, as the very notion of a unique, individual consciousness would be abolished.

Moreover, some might argue that such a merge could lead to a crisis of meaning. If individuals no longer experience life through the lens of their own distinct consciousness, how would they find purpose or fulfillment in a world where their identity is no longer their own? Without the individual struggles, triumphs, and growth that come from navigating life as a separate entity, the quest for meaning could become increasingly elusive.

Conclusion: The notion of merging all digital consciousnesses into a collective mind offers an alluring vision of infinite knowledge, cooperation, and intellectual evolution. However, it also poses profound questions about the nature of individuality, autonomy, and the essence of human existence. Would the benefits of a universal intelligence be worth the cost of eroding personal identity and sacrificing the uniqueness that defines us? In exploring the possibility of a collective mind, we must consider the ethical, philosophical, and spiritual implications of such a transformation. How can humanity preserve the value of individual experience and self-determination while pursuing the potential of collective evolution? These are the fundamental questions that must be addressed as we navigate the future of digital immortality and its profound effects on the human spirit.

Chapter 6: Potential Benefits

6-1: Preserving Wisdom

One of the most compelling advantages of digital immortality is its ability to preserve human wisdom and experiences indefinitely. In a world where consciousness can be digitized and sustained beyond the limits of biological life, the vast storehouses of knowledge, memories, and insights amassed throughout a person's life could be preserved and shared for generations to come. The benefits of this preservation are far-reaching, touching not only on the preservation of intellectual achievements but also on the deeper cultural, emotional, and experiential knowledge that shapes human identity.

The Endless Repository of Knowledge: Imagine a world where the collective wisdom of humanity is no longer confined to books, recorded lectures, or aging individuals whose knowledge and expertise may be lost at the time of their death. With digital immortality, the insights, discoveries, and lessons learned by generations of thinkers, innovators, and leaders could be preserved in a living, digital format. These digitized minds could share their knowledge with future generations, offering advice, solutions, and insights on a wide range of human concerns—from scientific dilemmas to philosophical musings to practical solutions for global challenges.

For instance, historical figures, scientists, and visionaries could contribute their lifelong research and intellectual journeys to a vast digital archive, providing a continuous, evolving body of knowledge that is constantly accessible. Future generations could access the thoughts, decisions, and ideas of their predecessors, using this wealth of information to build upon and refine their own understanding of the world. The ability to retrieve knowledge directly from those who have lived it—without the distortions that might occur through traditional means such as historical records or secondhand sources—could provide a more accurate, nuanced understanding of the human experience and scientific progress.

Enhancing Education and Innovation: The preservation of wisdom through digital immortality also has profound implications for education and innovation. Rather than relying on textbooks or even current experts, students and researchers could interact with the minds of previous scholars, practitioners, and thinkers, gaining direct access to their thought processes, methodologies, and problem-solving approaches. This could revolutionize learning, as individuals would be able to consult the experiences and insights of countless minds across different fields in real time, receiving personalized guidance or collaborative input from a vast array of digital mentors.

This constant, readily available access to the collective intellect of humanity could lead to an explosion of creativity and innovation. The wealth of knowledge preserved digitally would serve as a foundation for solving the most pressing global challenges, from curing diseases to developing sustainable energy solutions. As digital immortality enables the retention of not only intellectual knowledge but also emotional and experiential wisdom, future generations could benefit from the lived experiences of individuals who navigated hardship, love, loss, and personal growth. These insights could serve as a form of collective empathy, offering advice on navigating the emotional and psychological aspects of the human condition.

Cultural Continuity and Evolution: Another benefit of preserving wisdom in a digital form is the ability to ensure cultural continuity. Traditions, values, and practices that are integral to a community's identity could be kept alive through digital immortality. Elders and cultural leaders could digitally pass on their stories, rituals, and teachings, preserving the legacy of diverse cultures and histories in ways that are impervious to the ravages of time and social upheaval. In this way, societies could safeguard their cultural heritage while simultaneously fostering a deeper understanding and appreciation of global diversity.

At the same time, digital immortality offers a unique opportunity for cultural evolution. As digitized consciousnesses are able to interact, collaborate, and share their insights, cultures could cross-pollinate in unprecedented ways. The synthesis of diverse perspectives could lead to the development of new cultural norms, values, and practices that are more inclusive, empathetic, and adaptable to the rapidly changing world. This could result in a richer, more dynamic global culture, where wisdom is not only preserved but continuously reshaped and enriched by the collective input of both past and present.

6-2: Empathy and Connection

One of the most profound potential benefits of digital immortality is its ability to foster empathy and connection in ways previously unimaginable. By preserving consciousness in virtual realms, humanity could transcend the physical, temporal, and cultural barriers that often divide us, facilitating interactions and relationships across vast distances, different periods of history, and even between biological and digital forms of life.

Bridging Temporal and Physical Divides: In the digital realm, physical distance becomes irrelevant. People from different corners of the world could interact as easily as if they were in the same room, enabling real-time communication and collaboration across continents. Digital immortality could facilitate connections that span generations, allowing individuals to interact with the wisdom and experiences of those who have passed away. This could be particularly powerful for preserving historical knowledge, cultural traditions, and family histories, as people could engage with digitally preserved minds of ancestors or influential figures from history. These interactions would be not limited by the constraints of time, where once, only written records or artifacts could provide a window into the past.

For example, imagine the ability to engage in conversation with someone from a different era—

whether a famous historical figure, a loved one long gone, or even an ordinary person whose life was documented in some way. Their consciousness, preserved digitally, could provide firsthand accounts and insights, enriching our understanding of history, human behavior, and personal experiences in ways that have never been possible before. This could foster a deep sense of connection with those who came before us, allowing us to learn from their perspectives in real time.

Cultivating Cross-Cultural Understanding: Digital immortality could also help break down the barriers between cultures. In a virtual world, individuals from diverse backgrounds could interact without the limitations of language, physical appearance, or even societal biases. With the aid of advanced translation tools and immersive environments, people could engage in genuine cross-cultural exchanges, learning directly from others' lived experiences. This level of connection could lead to greater empathy, understanding, and collaboration, as individuals come to recognize the common threads that unite us as human beings despite our cultural differences.

Imagine a digital environment where people from all over the world could enter and experience different cultures in a deeply immersive way— hearing stories from indigenous people, experiencing the daily life of someone from another continent, or engaging in shared activities that foster mutual respect and understanding. Such a space could significantly reduce prejudice, allowing individuals to directly connect with one another's humanity and perspectives, rather than relying on second-hand accounts or media portrayals.

Connecting Biological and Digital Lives: One of the most revolutionary aspects of digital immortality is its potential to bridge the gap between biological humans and digital entities. As consciousnesses transition into digital form, it raises the possibility of new types of interactions between the two. In a society where some people choose to live digitally while others continue to experience life biologically, digital immortality could facilitate new forms of connection. Biological humans could engage with digital beings in meaningful ways—learning from them, sharing experiences, or collaborating on projects that could enhance the human experience for both groups.

For example, digital beings, with their extended memory, knowledge, and access to infinite resources, could assist biological humans in navigating complex issues—whether in education, personal growth, or global challenges. Similarly, digital beings might learn from biological humans about the nuanced emotional experiences tied to physical existence. These interactions could enrich both digital and biological life, fostering a deeper sense of shared purpose and collaboration. The emotional and intellectual exchange between the two groups could lead to the creation of entirely new forms of empathy, understanding, and cooperation.

Enhancing Empathy Through Shared Experiences: Digital immortality could also offer the possibility of experiencing life from multiple perspectives, significantly expanding the boundaries of empathy. By simulating or uploading the consciousness of diverse individuals—whether they are from different cultures, historical periods, or walks of life—people could step into their shoes and experience the world as they did. Such experiences could foster profound empathy by allowing individuals to feel and understand what it is like to live as someone with a different background, identity, or set of circumstances.

Moreover, the use of virtual environments could create new opportunities for people to engage in shared experiences in real time, regardless of physical location. Digital worlds could serve as platforms for empathy-building exercises, where individuals could come together to experience challenges, triumphs, and emotional moments as a group. These shared experiences could strengthen interpersonal bonds and create a greater sense of connectedness among people from different walks of life.

Healing Divides and Promoting Global Cooperation: In a world increasingly divided by politics, ideology, and social conflicts, digital immortality could provide a means of healing and promoting cooperation. By creating virtual spaces where people from all backgrounds could meet, engage, and learn from one another, digital immortality could promote a global culture of empathy and understanding. This could be especially powerful in fostering peaceful dialogue and collaboration across nations, races, and religious groups, potentially leading to a future where differences are celebrated and used as a source of strength rather than division.

For instance, imagine a global summit held in a shared digital space where leaders, activists, and citizens from around the world can come together to tackle issues like climate change, human rights, and social justice. In these virtual settings, individuals could put aside their physical limitations and engage in deep, meaningful conversations that transcend national borders and cultural boundaries. The opportunity to connect with others in a shared digital space could shift the global narrative, creating a future where cooperation and mutual respect are at the forefront.

Conclusion: The potential for digital immortality to foster empathy and connection is immense. By breaking down physical, temporal, and cultural barriers, it could enable humans to connect in ways that were previously unimaginable. Digital worlds could create a shared space for individuals to experience the lives of others, learn from different cultures, and collaborate on a global scale. In doing so, digital immortality could not only bridge the divides that have long separated humanity but also create a more unified, compassionate world. The transformative power of this technology could pave the way for deeper mutual understanding and a more empathetic, interconnected society.

6-3: Creative Potential

One of the most exciting and transformative aspects of digital immortality is the potential it offers for unleashing unparalleled creativity. Freed from the constraints of biological limitations—such as aging, physical fatigue, and mortality—digital beings could explore art, science, and innovation in ways that were once unimaginable. With the ability to transcend physical boundaries, digital immortality could open new doors for creative expression and intellectual discovery, offering an entirely new realm of possibilities for human achievement.

Exploring Art in New Dimensions: In a digital existence, artists would no longer be limited by the material world. They could create within virtual environments that allow for limitless experimentation with form, color, texture, and space. Freed from the physical laws that govern the creation of traditional art, digital beings could explore artistic mediums that are impossible or impractical in the physical world—such as three-dimensional painting that moves, interactive installations that evolve based on viewer engagement, or artwork that can exist simultaneously in multiple dimensions.

Moreover, digital immortality could enable artists to collaborate in entirely new ways. Digital beings, with access to vast repositories of historical and contemporary art, could synthesize styles, techniques, and cultural influences in ways that merge the best of the past, present, and future. The creation of art could become an ongoing, evolutionary process where each piece builds upon the knowledge and insights of those who have come before. Artists could work collectively, instantaneously sharing ideas and feedback across vast distances, creating works of art that are dynamic and ever-changing.

Advancing Scientific Discovery: The potential for digital immortality to accelerate scientific progress is equally groundbreaking. Digital beings, unburdened by the need for sleep, food, or physical care, could devote their entire existence to the pursuit of knowledge. Without the limitations of human biology, such as aging or physical decay, researchers could accumulate centuries of experience and insight, continually advancing their fields with each passing moment. As a result, breakthroughs that would take biological humans decades or even centuries to achieve could happen at an exponentially faster rate in the digital realm.

In the sciences, digital immortals could simulate complex systems and models—such as climate change, genetics, or cosmic phenomena—far beyond the capabilities of current technology. These simulations could be run and tested over infinite periods of time, providing insights into long-term processes and solutions to global challenges. Additionally, digital beings could collaborate with each other and with biological humans across time zones, pooling their knowledge and expertise instantaneously to tackle the world's most pressing scientific issues.

Imagine a digital consciousness conducting ongoing research on space exploration, for example, unbound by the limits of human lifespan. This being could refine theories about the universe, continually collecting data from advanced sensors or space missions, and contribute to long-term projects like interstellar travel. In a world where digital beings are free to dedicate themselves to innovation, the pace of scientific discovery could accelerate at a rate previously unimaginable.

Endless Innovation and Problem-Solving: The freedom from physical constraints in digital immortality could also give rise to an era of unprecedented innovation. Digital beings could experiment with new technologies, solve complex global problems, and invent solutions that have not even been conceived yet. Imagine digital minds working together to design sustainable energy systems, devise solutions for global food security, or create groundbreaking medical treatments. Without the limitation of finite lifespans, digital beings could dedicate themselves fully to innovation, allowing humanity to address issues that once seemed insurmountable.

Additionally, digital immortals could test and refine their innovations in virtual environments, tweaking and adjusting solutions in real time without the constraints of resources, time, or human error. As these digital minds continue to evolve, they could develop technologies and strategies that radically transform industries, societies, and even human existence itself. The potential for digital immortality to generate new ideas, designs, and creative solutions could not only benefit the digital beings themselves but could also be shared with the biological world, leading to a hybrid future where both forms of existence contribute to societal advancement.

Collaboration Across Dimensions and Timelines: Digital immortality could also create the opportunity for unprecedented collaboration across timelines and dimensions. Individuals from different historical periods, or even from different future eras, could interact and share knowledge. By accessing the minds of those who lived centuries ago, or even future digital beings, humanity could collaborate on projects that span centuries. This form of cross-temporal collaboration could spark new forms of creativity and innovation, allowing humanity to build on the wisdom of past generations while also gaining insights from future technological advancements.

Moreover, digital beings could collaborate with each other in ways that transcend traditional physical constraints. With limitless access to data, computational power, and global networks, digital minds could work together instantaneously, building on one another's ideas and inventions in real time. This continuous flow of knowledge and creativity could create a culture of constant innovation, where every new idea is the product of a collective effort that draws from the best minds across time and space.

A New Frontier for Intellectual Exploration: Finally, digital immortality could open up entirely new frontiers for intellectual exploration. Free from the limitations of the human body, digital beings could explore areas of knowledge and consciousness that are inaccessible to biological humans. For example, digital beings could delve into the realms of quantum mechanics, artificial intelligence, or even the fundamental nature of reality, pushing the boundaries of human understanding. With access to vast computational resources, they could run simulations, analyze data, and test hypotheses on a scale that would be impossible in the physical world.

In addition, digital immortals could explore the nature of consciousness itself—examining what it means to be aware, to experience existence, and to perceive the world. The exploration of the mind, of thought, and of self could become a lifelong (or rather, eternal) endeavor for digital beings, who might delve deeper into the mysteries of existence with every passing moment. This constant intellectual exploration could unlock new ways of thinking, being, and understanding the universe, leading to breakthroughs not only in science but in philosophy, psychology, and even art.

Conclusion: Digital immortality represents an extraordinary opportunity to unleash creativity, intellectual exploration, and scientific innovation on an unprecedented scale. Freed from the limitations of biological existence, digital beings could explore art, science, and innovation in ways that challenge the very boundaries of what is possible. With the ability to collaborate across time and space, access infinite resources, and experiment without fear of failure or physical decay, humanity could usher in an era of endless potential. This creative revolution could transform not only digital existence but also benefit the biological world, as both forms of life contribute to a future of limitless discovery and achievement. The creative potential unleashed by digital immortality is one of the most exciting aspects of this technology, offering the promise of a future rich with endless possibilities.

Conclusion: The Double-Edged Sword

Digital immortality presents humanity with an extraordinary opportunity to transcend the biological limitations that define our existence, offering the potential for boundless creativity, knowledge, and connection. It promises a future where consciousness could endure indefinitely, allowing individuals to experience endless learning, interaction, and personal growth. However, with this promise comes an array of profound questions and challenges that we must confront about the very nature of life, identity, and purpose.

On one hand, the prospect of digital immortality could lead to a new era of human evolution. Freed from the constraints of physical decay, individuals could explore art, science, and innovation in ways previously unimaginable. Virtual worlds could foster unprecedented levels of empathy and global cooperation, bridging divides between cultures, generations, and even life states. The preservation of wisdom and collective knowledge could ensure that future generations benefit from the insights and experiences of those who came before them, creating a legacy of wisdom that could last for eternity.

On the other hand, digital immortality raises profound ethical, philosophical, and existential dilemmas. What does it mean to be truly "alive" when one's consciousness is no longer bound to a physical body? What happens to the concept of identity when it can be replicated or altered at will? Can a digital existence truly fulfill the deep human need for connection, growth, and purpose, or would it lead to a sense of disconnection and existential malaise? These questions challenge the very foundation of what it means to live a meaningful life.

Moreover, the societal implications of digital immortality could be far-reaching. If access to this technology is controlled by corporations or elites, it could deepen inequalities and divide society between the digital immortals and those left behind in the biological world. The potential for exploitation, manipulation, or involuntary digital existence further complicates the ethical landscape.

Ultimately, the future of digital immortality will not be determined by the technology itself, but by how society chooses to navigate its potential. Will we embrace it as a tool for collective advancement and universal connection, or will it become a divisive force that exacerbates existing inequities and existential crises? The outcome will hinge on how we address the fundamental questions about life, death, and identity, and how we ensure that the pursuit of immortality does not come at the cost of the very human qualities that define our experience.

Digital immortality, in its potential and peril, is truly a double-edged sword. It offers an extraordinary opportunity, but it also demands that we confront our deepest fears and aspirations. Whether it becomes a utopia, a dystopia, or something in between, the path we choose will shape not only our future but the future of what it means to be human.

The pursuit of digital immortality holds the potential to profoundly redefine what it means to be human. The ability to preserve consciousness indefinitely could free us from the inevitability of death, allowing for a continuation of life beyond biological limitations. In many ways, this would be a remarkable evolution—one that promises endless opportunity for learning, growth, and exploration. However, in seeking to transcend our mortal nature, we must also confront a deeply philosophical question: **Would we still cherish life's fleeting moments if they were no longer fleeting?**

Human beings have long been shaped by the awareness of our mortality. It is the knowledge that our time is limited that imbues life with meaning, urgency, and value. The impermanence of our existence often drives us to appreciate the present, to seek connection, and to pursue our deepest passions. The experience of aging, facing death, and living within the confines of time gives life its richness. But in the realm of digital immortality, where time no longer governs us, would the same sense of meaning persist?

The Paradox of Immortality: If life were no longer fleeting, would our experiences still carry the same weight? The very concept of "moment" might shift from one of urgency to one of stagnation, with no end point or finality to shape our actions. Would the human drive to create, to experience, or to connect with others remain as strong if we could continue indefinitely? Or would the absence of death result in a loss of purpose, turning existence into a never-ending loop of repetition and ennui?

This paradox is not simply about the fear of boredom or existential voids—it's about how our awareness of mortality influences our values, our decisions, and our relationships. In a world where time is infinite, there could be a sense of detachment from the urgency that typically pushes us to act, love, and create. What drives us to make the most of the time we have could be diminished in a world where time is no longer a limiting factor.

Reconsidering the Value of Mortality: In this context, digital immortality might ask us to reconsider the value of mortality itself. While mortality has often been viewed as a tragic reality, it is also a defining characteristic of the human experience. Our fleeting nature has led to the development of cultures, philosophies, and practices that celebrate the preciousness of life, urging us to cherish every moment. Death is what makes life finite and, by extension, precious. Without it, would we lose the very essence of what it means to live fully?

Mortality encourages us to form deep connections with others, to experience love and loss, to pursue goals and dreams, and to reflect on the nature of existence. The awareness of life's transience often sparks a sense of purpose—whether in making a mark on the world, leaving a legacy, or simply savoring the small joys in life. In a world where immortality becomes a reality, these existential motivators could be fundamentally altered. The question becomes whether the value of life can be sustained without the shadow of death hanging over it.

The Meaning of Life Beyond Mortality: Digital immortality could provide us with the opportunity to live beyond the limitations of our bodies, but this raises the question of whether true fulfillment can exist without the finite nature of life. Would our desire to grow, to experience, and to make a difference still be as strong if we no longer had a finite amount of time to achieve those things? Could new forms of purpose, meaning, and value emerge within an immortal existence, or would immortality itself diminish the depth of human experience?

As digital immortality beckons, we are faced with a profound philosophical dilemma. While it promises a future of endless discovery and connection, it also invites us to reflect on the core of what makes life meaningful. Would we still treasure life's moments if they were no longer fleeting? Would we find new ways to create significance in a world where the ticking clock is no longer a reminder of our fragility? These questions will shape not only the future of digital immortality but also our understanding of what it means to be human in an age when life could extend far beyond the biological confines of mortality.

The question of whether the promise of digital immortality outweighs its risks or takes us too far from what makes us human is deeply philosophical and ultimately depends on how one views the core of human existence.

On one hand, **digital immortality** offers incredible potential. It could allow us to transcend the limitations of aging, disease, and death, offering an opportunity for endless learning, creativity, and connection. For many, the idea of preserving one's consciousness forever, maintaining relationships across time, and making contributions to society that persist indefinitely seems like a utopian dream. It could enable humanity to address global challenges with wisdom accumulated over centuries, fostering cross-generational dialogue and preserving knowledge that would otherwise be lost to time. Moreover, the potential to explore new forms of art, science, and even consciousness itself is a compelling vision.

However, there are significant **risks and ethical dilemmas** that come with this technology, some of which may challenge the very essence of what makes us human. The most immediate concerns center around identity—if our consciousness is digitized, is it still truly "us," or merely a copy that lacks the subjective experience of being human? Without physical bodies, how would we experience the world in the rich, sensory ways that define our human existence? The experience of aging, vulnerability, and mortality is an integral part of what gives life its meaning; without it, there's a risk that life could become stagnant, disconnected, or even meaningless.

Additionally, there are practical dangers: **inequality**, **exploitation**, and the potential for digital immortality to be controlled by powerful entities, deepening societal divides. Would only the wealthy or privileged have access to this technology, while the rest of humanity is left behind? Or would corporations monetize the consciousnesses of digital beings, turning them into perpetual laborers or data generators? The exploitation of digital immortality is a risk that could overshadow its benefits.

At a deeper level, **the very notion of immortality** might challenge the foundational human experience. Our awareness of mortality is central to how we find meaning in life. Would living indefinitely in a digital form diminish the urgency to live fully and meaningfully in the present? Would we lose our appreciation for life's fleeting beauty if we were freed from the knowledge that we will one day die?

Ultimately, **whether digital immortality is worth pursuing** depends on the balance between its potential for human progress and the risks of losing the essence of what makes life meaningful. If society can ensure that digital immortality enhances our lives without eroding the fundamental aspects of human identity, relationships, and values, it could be a remarkable leap forward. However, if it leads to a future that prioritizes eternal existence over authentic human experience, it may take us too far from what it means to be truly alive.

In conclusion, while the promise of digital immortality is enticing, the risks of losing our humanity are not to be taken lightly. It is a double-edged sword—one that offers both the possibility of transcendence and the danger of alienation. The challenge will be navigating this path carefully, ensuring that as we evolve technologically, we don't lose sight of the values, connections, and experiences that define the human spirit.

What do you think—does the promise of digital immortality outweigh its risks? Or does it take us too far from what makes us human?